VIEW FROM A BENCH

A former headteacher, John Roper now lives and writes by the sea in Eastbourne. This is his first collection.

CONTENTS

VIEW FROM A BENCH

On my birthday, summer is delivered
to my door with the London Times. By ten
the sun is a fiery yolk in a pan
of blue, as beyond the road the gardener
swings a hedgecutter, while her black dog
sprawls in the shade and watches like a boss.
On the coast road, motor coaches whisper by
filled with blue-rinsed ladies and blazered
gents
in straw hats. And in the boatyard, a sea
breeze shakes the metal masts of yachts
aching to be afloat – to take the slap
of wind and waves against their glassy hulls –
while I unwrap the gift of standing still.

TO A GREYHOUND

I smile to think my wicker limbed old hound
has more coats than me, as saddled like a
Deb, in padded Barbour with cord trim, she
does her hot coals dance on the parquet floor.

Held at the gate, butting the iron rails
her body tensed as if waiting for the bell,
then off along the straight towards the beach
delighting in the smells off grass and stone.

This last grey year of lockdown has taught me
some ways in which we seem to be the same:
a liking for biscuits and daytime naps,
the feeling that our best years are behind.

THREE POETS (Written after seeing Roger McGough)

I can count the poets I have met on
the fingers of one hand. First, was the coiffed
fur-coated lady, ushered like a queen
into the school hall, where crammed in tight
we
coughed and fidgeted with her stapled sheets

Second, a few years on, a student now
with satchel, scarf and beard, I heard a soft
voiced Cornish bard read from his collected
poems and later handed to him that night's
beer money as the price to take them home

Third, was last week, with covid mask to hand,
a poet with white hair like a wizard
who years back had dragged poetry, kicking
and
screaming, out from the stuffy salons and
into the cool streets and the crowded bars

THE WESTERN LAWNS

This town has been far out at sea all night
and the wind behind the morning tide still
power-hoses the beach, as thinking
on my father's wreck, I run under
the pier and travel west towards the
bandstand carrying an old rhyme:
'At Eastbourne this season, where shall I stay?
East of the pier dear, you never should stray.'
For now the hotels get bigger and
art-deco blocks of flats nod to them.
On the Western Lawns a new mechanical
wheel, spokes patterned like a paper
doily, dwarfs the ancient Wish Tower,
while at five minute intervals an empty
cable car hangs in nothing, like when
I was a child and spent each winter in the alps

THE PIER AT EASTBOURNE

Today a handwritten sign tells me
that the camera obscura is closed
for repairs, though its golden dome still
winks at strollers on the promenade.

Built on stilts that let the structure
roll in rough seas, the pier juts out from
a ribbon of hotels, skirting the shingle beach
and divides modest east from monied west

Its echoing slats have weathered wars, storms
and fires, but all is well today in the
tearoom, tables laid with snowy cloths and
the gift shop piled high with crested
keepsakes

The only sounds are a clack of coins from
the fruit machines and the swish of a
fishing line at the pierhead, where once
paddle steamers set out on trips to France.

I turn back towards the panorama
of the bay, a view my grandfather saw
caught in the camera obscura's curved
lens on his last summer before the war

THE GLASSBLOWER

In Neptune's orbit there is a comet
with a Diners Card number for a name
and a stubby tail like a rabbit,
heading for the earth in 2031.

Meanwhile, in his studio on the pier
the glassblower wields an orange
tail of burning gas, to sculpt
a flower from a pile of sand.

His goggle eyes big as a fly,
as like a stargazer he locks onto
the here and now, blind to
rumours from far flung galaxies

THE FOUNTAIN

Each Sunday, Mrs Curling would sit in her
paid oak pew, dressed in widow's hat and
coat,
unbowed by age, the wafer melting on
her tongue, thin dry lips stained wine red.

To mark her life she gave the town a
drinking fountain, forged by foundry
craftsmen
as a journey's break for man and horse,
a place to meet a friend or make a speech.

She believed God's word could quench a
lifelong
thirst, but it was the needlework she found
for poor deserving women, that nourished
their frail bodies through the hardest winter

THE BOAT

An upturned boat lurks halfway up the beach
a watermark to harness each high tide.
Baked black by the sun and soaked by showers
a few stray daisies climb its swollen hull.

In a world of aimless movement, it finds
some point in being still, and yet with each
slow circle of the sun, the timbers edge
a hair's breadth closer turning into coal

SONNET

There was a time when I had time to kill
But times have changed and now it's killing
me.
Blank diaries, I couldn't wait to fill
With things to do and brand new sights to see.

There was a time when I could run for miles,
These days I pause for breath en route to bed.
Each Friday night I'd go out on the tiles
My heart a country mile before my head.

There was a time when I had far to go
But now the view from here affords me joy,
The breakers from the sea in endless flow
A beach I used to play on as a boy

Please, Father Time defer the final bow
And keep alive this peace that's in me now

RUNNING MAN

My bathroom scales flash like a fruit machine,
as if the outcome is a turn of pitch
and toss, rather than a statement of the
fact that there is too much of me around.

And so my rubber souls add backbeat to
the rhythm of the waves, as panting like a
train
I pass walkers in their day-glo cagoules
off for the set-lunch at The Bay Hotel.

With pistol pumping arms I reach the pier
And for a talisman stretch to tag its
rusted struts. A man on the move again
digging for meaning in pursuit of less

ON PRINCES PARK LAKE

On the lake today a speedboat motor
whines a warning to the snowy swans,
a gaudy toy, sent slicing across the
lake's diameter by the man on the bank, with
a beer gut and a backwards baseball cap.

By the sluice gates that feed the lake
with sea water, a boy with floppy hair
in fleece and shorts, teaches his excited
young students how to tack into the wind.

Years back, they had boats for hire and one
golden summer, as a child of ten, I left behind
the pedal boats and learnt to row, like the
Swallows and Amazons in the books I read

MR EASTBOURNE

Hidden on a street of shady trees, the house
bears a blue plaque that reads: 'The man
they called Mr Eastbourne once lived here.'

It stands a sunny evening stroll from the
theatre on the pier, where his Summer
Starlight Show played for twenty years.

My father took us one August night, half
remembered from thirties radio shows,
he was pleased to find him just the same

A catch phrase and a faded back-cloth,
his vent act with a vacant painted doll
then the small band played his song.

He sold eight million discs that earned a
penny a side, enough to buy four streets
of smart villas a short walk from the pier.

MAY DAY

To mark the holiday, a slice of sun
like lemon in the frosted glass of gin
served to shining ones, set apart like stars,
high on the terrace of The Grand Hotel.

While below, the promenade fills with men
grown weary from months of furlough, with fat
wife and muscled dog in tow, determined
to squeeze a drop of pleasure from the day.

For by the sugar scented pier, neon
signs flash orders to stay in groups of six
to keep infections low, while overhead
the seagulls glide like freedom in the sky

MACKEREL MOSAIC

Today, the sea is a bubbling cauldron
full of mackerel, come to feast on
the silvery whitebait carpet, tossed
like wriggling trash, onto the pebbled beach.

Gulls gather in a squadron cloud
over the mill pond sea, while for us
at the top of the food chain, it's a day
to eat ice cream and fat chips undisturbed

L'AUTEUR

When her husband has gone to work, Nicole
colours canvas in her sun filled attic
studio until noon, when she walks on
the promenade with a small flat-faced dog.

Some days she meets a friend for lunch. Salad
Nicoise with a crisp white wine, but often
she eats alone, shrouded in shades at a
pavement café and reads a book by Sartre.

To hold ennui at bay, she has lately
brokered a lover and on Thursdays they
meet to tangle limbs in a rented room,
then smoke and bicker about art and life.

Wednesdays, she visits the cinema
a bijou club in a deep cellar bar,
because French black and white, subtitled new
wave films have become her raison d'etre

HOTEL CHATSWORTH

Built to look like a wedding cake,
the hotel's front, sandblasted the
colour of honey, glows in the sun.

Its name, picked out in royal blue letters,
is a nod to the English duke who planned
this town two centuries back.

A grand resort, architect designed in the
continental style with terraces and parks,
built by gentlemen for gentlemen.

At the foot of the stone steps a glass case
displays no pictures or prices, just as
the seventh duke would have wanted

FUSCIARDI'S

Spoken with a soft cee, as in fuchsia
this café on Eastbourne's seafront
first made ice cream the year that
Sergeant Pepper made the charts.

A glazed tile front draws the eye inside
to polished chrome and the hiss of steam,
with a gelato rainbow ranged in tubs, the
recipes passed down like family jewels.

Behind the counter glide the full skirted
smiling ladies. Dressed all in black
they conjure frozen sculpted art
from ice cream, sauce and shards of fruit.

I first went there as a boy, after a
morning on the beach, chasing a slick of
ice cream round a steel dish, while my parents
tried croissants and drank coffee from glass
cups

DINING ALFRESCO

They have extra security today
at the café on the beach.
To keep away the pushy gulls
a cut-out kite circles on a line,
pitching and weaving in the salt wind
like a tribute act, boldly aping the real thing.

But the seagulls are convinced
and take their custom elsewhere
so alfresco diners can eat in peace,
as can the stout undercover pigeons
that march across the decking and
seem content to feast on crumbs

BANDSTAND

September mist still hangs above the sea,
but the sun is high enough to spot-weld
a circle in the bandstand's blue domed roof
and dapple the blue balconies of this
thirties tribute to the Neo-Grec school.

By the ice cream hutch, a throaty busker
strums and sings about a blind man and a
road, while on the half-circle stage, jet black
against the sunlight, the brass players shift
chairs and unpack their awkward instruments.

In the summer, there are weekend tribute
shows from Abba to The Zombies and each
Wednesday, Peter Tchaikovsky with fireworks,
but this September Sunday there's only
ice cream, a busker and a silver band

AZIMUTH

The posts of Azimuth guard the shore,
made from greenheart timbers
that ruled the waves, when wooden ships
first beached at Pevensey.
Now rescued from the sea's wet jaws
they are the ribs of extinct behemoths,
lost mastheads from a fleet sent out by Spain,
or marker stones for those who sadly
never reached the sanctuary of home

AT BEACHY HEAD

The bones of a young woman are uncovered
by the blood and bandage striped lighthouse.
Her teeth reveal a diet of fish from the sea
and berries plucked from bushes that smother
the wet grasslands above the cliffs.
She arrived here back two thousand years,
landed on this beach with members of her
tribe.
Explorers from a sub-Saharan land, they
stepped ashore with hand held out to meet a
friend

AFTER RAIN

At the beach café a canvas
sheet hangs like a shroud over
stacks of silver chairs and piles of
mottled wet leaves block up the drains.

The creeper on your balcony
is overgrown but there is often a
light showing in the bedroom
you planned to paint in white and gold.

These are the days of missing you,
as this year August did not stay
to lift November and streets hang
empty as sometimes after rain

A HOME BY THE SEA

The waves hiss against shingle, as upholstered
in scarf and coat, his back parade ground
straight,
he walks to the café for a pot of Assam tea
no milk and a toasted teacake without jam.

Then sits at the window by the windswept
veranda
joined by ghosts that tumble and twist like
smoke.
A short marriage, long years of chalk and
registration,
his mother's grey viduity, then back here
to his childhood home by the sea.

He walks along the promenade and finds an
empty bench, with a clear view of the ocean.
It has, 'He loved the sea' etched in rusted
metal
below the faded letters of his own name

A BOOKSHOP IDYLL

Today it seems the dust in Camilla's Bookshop
dates from when my mother was a girl, as
masked up
like a surgeon, I tread down the book
encrusted stair
to the tomblike subterranean stacks, where

the rows of orphaned poetry books are there
interred from Amis to Zephaniah, though
I've never yet made it past poor Sylvia Plath,
without the need to surface for a breath of air.

Camilla keeps a raucous parrot in a cage
and a picture from when punk rock was all the
rage.
I feed my bank card and the Life of Crow,
through
the gap in her covid plastic shield, and then
wait

for her to read the message on the title page:

'I won't be gone forever, think of me as I do you'

She tells me that poems have been popular of late,

at least with those like me who live next door to fate

Printed in Great Britain
by Amazon